WORLDWATCH REPORT 185

Green Economy and Green Jobs in China:
Current Status and Potentials for 2020

JIAHUA PAN, HAIBING MA,
AND YING ZHANG

LISA MASTNY, *EDITOR*

WORLDWATCH INSTITUTE

On the cover: Chinese workers install a wind turbine at Chicheng Wind Farm in Hebei province.
Photograph © Simon Lim/Greenpeace

Table of Contents

Acknowledgments

This report was written collaboratively by the Worldwatch Institute and the Institute for Urban & Environmental Studies (IUE) at the Chinese Academy of Social Sciences (CASS). The lead authors were Haibing Ma with Worldwatch and Dr. Jiahua Pan and Dr. Ying Zhang with CASS, with important additional contributions from Dr. Yang Zheng, Dr. Mou Wang, Mr. Changyi Liu, Ms. Mengmei Chen, and Mr. Bin Zhang. The report also benefited greatly from the comments and recommendations of numerous experts on China's green economy, with special thanks going to Professor Chenguang Pan (CASS), Dr. Shifa Ke (Beijing Forestry University), and Dr. Anhua Zhang for their careful review of early drafts.

At Worldwatch, we extend our appreciation to Christopher Flavin for his insightful comments in the early stages of the report. Robert Engelman served as internal reviewer and helped to enhance both the messages of the report and the way they were presented. We are also grateful for the committed support of Director of Institutional Relations Mary C. Redfern, Senior Editor Lisa Mastny, Director of Publications and Marketing Patricia Shyne, and Communications Director Russell Simon. The design and layout were completed skillfully by designer Lyle Rosbotham.

Finally, we are indebted to the Ministry for Foreign Affairs of Finland for its generous support of this project. It was a pleasure to work with the Ministry on this initiative.

About the Authors

Jiahua Pan is Deputy Director of the Institute for Urban & Environmental Studies at the Chinese Academy of Social Sciences (CASS). His research interests include the economic and social dimensions of sustainable development, energy and development, climate policy, and the economics of the environment and natural resources. Dr. Pan has also worked for the United Nations Development Programme's Beijing Office as an advisor on environment and development. He is a lead author of the IPCC Working Group III Third and Fourth Assessment Reports on Mitigation. He is also a member of the China National Expert Panel on Climate Change, an advisor to the China State Environmental Protection Administration, and serves as Vice President of the Chinese Society of Ecological Economists. Dr. Pan received his PhD at Cambridge University in 1992 and is the author of 150 papers and articles in academic journals, magazines, and newspapers in English or Chinese.

Haibing Ma is China Program Manager at the Worldwatch Institute. His priority research and management areas at Worldwatch are clean energy and climate change, including an initiative to explore green economy potentials and impacts in China. Ma is the main point of contact between the Institute and key stakeholders in China, including energy and climate officials and industry experts. Before coming to Worldwatch, Ma was an International Policy Associate at the Center for Clean Air Policy (CCAP), where he was involved in developing mitigation scenarios and implementation plans for China's electricity, iron and steel, and cement sectors; power-sector modeling; and drafting a low-carbon development plan for the transportation sector. Ma holds a B.A. in Public Administration from Zhejiang University in China and an M.A. in Public Policy Analysis from Beijing University.

Ying Zhang is a post-doctoral scholar at the Institute for Urban & Environmental Studies at the Chinese Academy of Social Sciences (CASS). She is also a research fellow with Research Center of Sustainable Development at the Joint Laboratory of CASS and CMA in Climate Change Economics Simulation. Dr. Zhang's main research interests include modeling work in climate change economics, quantitative economics, low-carbon development, and environmental economics. She received her doctoral and master's degrees in Economics at the Institute of Quantitative and Technical Economics at CASS, and earned B.A. and B.S. degrees in Economics and Applied Math from Wuhan University.

Summary

Over the past decade, and especially during the 11th Five-Year period of 2006–10, China has prioritized green development in almost all of its leading economic sectors. One of the greatest promises of China's green transition is the potential for expanded employment in industries and economic sectors that can help slow and possibly reduce the country's environmental impact. This report explores greening activities in three leading sectors of China's economy: energy, transportation, and forestry. In doing so, it aims to shed light on the current scale of investment and employment in these sectors and to offer estimates of potentials for 2020.

China's energy sector is heavily dependent on coal. Increasing the share of renewable energy in the country's energy mix would contribute significantly to reducing emissions and play a vital role in greening the energy supply. This report focuses on economic and employment prospects in three renewable energy sectors that are advancing rapidly in China: solar hot water, solar photovoltaics (PV), and wind power.

During the 11th Five-Year Period (2006–10), China's solar PV power sector generated some 2,700 direct jobs and 6,500 indirect jobs annually, on average. This is projected to increase to an average of 6,680 direct jobs and 16,370 indirect jobs annually between 2011 and 2020. Given the rapid growth in China's solar industry and potential upward revisions in government projections, these estimates for future green jobs could increase considerably in the coming years.

China's wind power industry—both the power generation and turbine manufacturing sectors—created an average of 40,000 direct green jobs annually between 2006 and 2010.

Divided highway and wind farm in Xinjiang province.

Even factoring in increased productivity, China's wind power development between 2011 and 2020 is projected to generate some 34,000 green jobs annually on average.

Formerly the "kingdom of bicycles," China is expected to add as many as 220 million new vehicles between now and 2020. This report focuses on economic and employment prospects in three green transportation subsectors: China's alternative-fuel vehicle industry (the development of hybrid cars and electric cars), the high-speed rail sector, and urban rail in Beijing.

Despite its relative newness, the Chinese market for alternatively fueled vehicles is expanding rapidly. By mid-2010, China was home to some 5,000 such vehicles, with a combined distance of just over 81 million kilometers traveled. If the government continues to prioritize the development of hybrid and electric vehicles during the 2011–20 period, cumulative production could reach 16.7 million, or an average of 1.67 million vehicles annually. This would lead to the creation of roughly 1.2 million green jobs annually in this sector, on average.

Already a world leader in high-speed rail (HSR) development, China aims to have 18,000 kilometers of HSR by 2020, which would create an average of 230,000 direct and 400,000 indirect jobs annually during the 2011–20 period, or a total of 630,000 jobs annually.

As one of the most populated cities in the world and still growing, Beijing's municipal government has stepped up its urban rail ambitions in recent years. Its current targets include completion of 660 kilometers of lines by 2015 (at a total investment of $77 billion) and construction of another 340 kilometers of lines during 2016–20 (at a total investment of $69 billion). This could bring more than 437,000 jobs each year by 2020.

On the forest resources front, China's forests are home to more than 1,800 species of wild animals, more than 2,000 tree species, and more than 6,000 species of bushes, hundreds of which are found only in China. Nourishing these forested areas is vital for sustaining the country's green transition. This report focuses on economic and employment prospects in three non-timber forestry subsectors: forestation, forest management, and forest tourism.

Although China does not have abundant forest resources, government-led forestation efforts have led to an impressive expansion in nationwide forest cover. Based on our estimation, the forestation sector employed as many as 1.8 million full-time workers in 2010 alone, or an average of 1.6 million workers annually during the 2005–10 period. To achieve its 2020 goals, China's forestation activities could offer as many as 1.1 million direct and indirect jobs annually during 2011–20. Managing the newly added forest area during this period would bring another 1 million jobs.

China also has great potential to expand its niche sector of forest park tourism, as the country is home to more than 2,000 forest parks nationwide. We estimate that by 2020, this relatively new green sector could provide 392,000 direct jobs and 607,000 indirect jobs, or nearly 1 million green jobs in total.

Due to the different methodologies used to derive green jobs estimates in this report, it may not be appropriate to simply add these estimates together to derive an overall green jobs figure for China. It can be stated with confidence, however, that the three sectors highlighted in the report—energy, transportation, and forestry—could provide at least 4.5 million green jobs in 2020. If these sectors continue their rapid expansion, and if similar estimates could be obtained for other emerging green sectors in China, it would be clear that the economy-wide potential for green jobs is enormous.

China has established a long-term green vision and will almost certainly meet or surpass its ambitious green economy goals. Yet vision alone is not enough; attention also needs to be paid to the actual steps being taken to achieve those goals. One of the greatest lessons to be learned from the early days of China's green transition is that building a sustainable future requires using approaches and processes that are sustainable in practice as well. To achieve that goal, the Chinese government needs to enhance its administrative efficiency and to adopt new market-based approaches to create a supportive yet stable environment for nourishing the green economy.

This report represents the most thorough effort known to date to explore China's green economy and green jobs potentials. In the future, the availability of more comprehensive and more reliable data will allow for an expansion and deepening of this effort, enabling Chinese policymakers and other stakeholders to better understand the options that are available to them in pursuing an effective green transition.

China's Shift to a Green Economy

China is in the early stages of a potentially earthshaking transition. The Chinese government recognizes that "greening" the economy is an emerging global aspiration and has embraced the strategic goal of boosting the country's economic growth while also enhancing environmental protection. Top Chinese political leaders have emphasized on many occasions that their country is committed to a green development path that is based on improved efficiency of energy and water use, shifts to renewable energy, and other critical steps.

At the 17th National Congress of the Chinese Communist Party in 2007, President Hu Jintao stated that "implementation of the scientific concept of development must rely on comprehensive, coordinated, and sustainable development."[1]* At other high-level occasions, including the 2010 APEC Summit in Yokohama, Japan, President Hu affirmed that China seeks to transform its growth pattern and to engage in greener, more sustainable development.[2] Vice Premier Li Keqiang has similarly noted that China "must nurture and strengthen a green economy, promote green development," and foster the necessary institutional arrangements to create both policy incentives and standards for doing so.[3]

China's shift to a greener economy provides an opportunity to create new pathways for economic growth, including through the creation of "green jobs."† But it also reflects the need to address serious environmental problems that have resulted from decades of rapid economic development. China's gross domestic product (GDP) has grown by an average of 10 percent annually during the last three decades—among the fastest rates in the world.[4] During the second quarter of 2010, China passed Japan to become the world's second largest economy.[5] The rapid industrial development required for this growth has left a heavy environmental toll.

Since the 1980s, China has been plagued by worsening air pollution from coal burning and other industrial sources. From the late 1990s to the mid-2000s, more than 60 percent of Chinese cities, home to two-thirds of the country's urban population, failed to meet the national Environmental and Air Quality Standard.[6] In 2008, the World Health Organization listed seven Chinese cities, including the capital city Beijing, as among the "10 most polluted places" in the world.[7] The Chinese Academy of Social Sciences has estimated that air pollution accounts for as much as 16 percent of the economic toll caused by the country's environmental problems.[8]

Chinese greenhouse gas emissions are rising rapidly as well. In 2006, China passed the United States to become the world's largest emitter of carbon dioxide (CO_2) from industrial sources, primarily from fossil fuel combustion.[9] Roughly 80 percent of Chinese CO_2 emissions are from the burning of coal for power generation and other uses.[10] One of the dirtiest fossil fuels, coal accounts for nearly 70 percent of China's total energy consumption and was the source of 80 percent of the country's power generation between 2002 and 2008.[11]

Rapid industrialization has polluted China's

---

* Endnotes are grouped by section and begin on page 28.
† The terms "green economy" and "green jobs" have never been well or precisely defined. For the purposes of this report, a green economy refers to an economy that has made a significant shift toward producing economic value with less environmental impact; green jobs are jobs that are brought into being entirely or largely through this transformative economic process.

water resources. By 2005, some 59 percent of the country's rivers were considered undrinkable, based on the standard set by the State Environmental Protection Agency (SEPA).[12] That same year, more than 70 percent of inland lakes and water reserves were considered heavily polluted and one-quarter of underground aquifers were deemed polluted, with more than half of urban aquifers heavily polluted.[13] Severe water pollution posed health risks to more than 360 million Chinese in 2005.[14]

Coal-fired power plant in Shuozhou, Shanxi province.

China's rural environment and land-based ecosystems are also suffering. By 2008, heavy metals, the bulk of them from industrial sources, were polluting one-fifth of the country's arable land, reducing the grain yield by an average of 10 million tons annually.[15*] With the reduction in arable land, China's per capita grain stocks dropped from 412 kilograms in 1998 to 334 kilograms in 2003.[16] Between 1994 and 2009, the annual rate of desertification increased from some 2,500 square kilometers to 3,500 square kilometers, costing the country an average of 54 billion yuan (US$8.3 billion) annually.[17†]

Human pressures and the explosive growth

* Units of measure throughout this report are metric unless common usage dictates otherwise.
† All dollar and cent amounts are expressed in U.S. dollars. Currencies in this report are converted at the rate of 1 U.S. dollar = 6.5 Chinese yuan.

of China's economy have likewise taken a toll on wildlife in the country. China is currently home to 156 of the 640 endangered species listed in the Convention on International Trade in Endangered Species of Wild Fauna and Flora (CITES).[18] Meanwhile, an estimated 15–20 percent of high-elevation plants nationwide are under threat due to forest loss and reduced ecosystem function.[19]

Overall, SEPA estimates that environmental damage cost China roughly 10 percent of its GDP in 2005.[20] Analysts have suggested that the country will need to spend at least 2 percent of its GDP to clean up 30 years of industrial waste.[21] All of these environmental challenges point to the need for a sweeping revision of China's development paradigm, a need now recognized by both the Communist Party and the government that it directs.

China is hardly the only country embracing a green economy. Its neighbor to the east, South Korea, stands out among several nations that have begun to adopt "green growth" initiatives or plans. Building on its success in developing more eco-conscious technologies, in 2010 South Korea launched a pathbreaking Green Growth Initiative that aims to transform the country from a resource- and carbon-intensive economy to one based on the efficient use of energy and resources. More than any other country in the world, South Korea has elevated the attainment of a green economy to the level of national strategy and launched a comprehensive institutional system for implementation.

South Korea's green growth initiative presents valuable lessons for both China and the rest of the developing world. Led by president Lee Myung-Bak, the strategy has gained broad public support, including from the major opposition party, and is being implemented through detailed and forceful legislation. Despite early opposition from the steel and cement industries, the initiative has been largely embraced by South Korea's major companies. Firms such as Hyundai and Samsung have responded by creating their own green growth strategies, including entering into new business areas such as solar and wind power, electric vehicles, and zero-emission factories. The government has also created a Global Green Growth Institute with the aim of scaling up financial and technical support to help other developing countries create their own green growth strategies and policies.

Although China's strategy is not as comprehensive as South Korea's, many Chinese policies and actions—both ongoing and planned—are clearly in line with the green growth paradigm. Over the past decade, and especially during the 11th Five-Year planning period of 2006–10, China has prioritized green development in almost all leading economic sectors. Efforts have been undertaken to boost energy efficiency in industry, transportation, and buildings; to develop wind, solar, and other renewable energy sources; to create a resource-saving "circular" economy; and to transform traditional sectors through the use of energy-efficient and environmentally sound technologies.

Yet China's green economy potential has barely been tapped. The United Nations Environment Programme (UNEP) defines a green economy as one that "results in improved human well-being and social equity, while significantly reducing environmental risks and ecological scarcities."[22] Although China should aim to meet all of these goals, in practice it is clear that establishing a green economy requires thinking more in "shades of green" than in absolute terms. China currently is in a transition period during which new green sectors, such as renewable energy and electric vehicles, co-exist with old "brown" industries, such as coal-based power.

One of the greatest promises of China's green transition is the potential for expanded employment in industries and economic sectors that promise to reduce or at least slow the country's environmental impact. Often called "green jobs" but ill-defined in practice, paid positions in such industries and sectors are increasingly available to jobseekers in China. As elsewhere, such opportunities are particularly important at a time of global economic uncertainty, when any job is an asset.

Although China's official unemployment rate has remained low—in urban areas, it has been below 5 percent for more than two decades—actual joblessness may be much higher.[23] According to a report from the Chinese Academy of Social Sciences, urban unemployment reached 9.4 percent in 2008.[24] Meanwhile, estimates put

surplus rural labor at more than 100 million people.[25] As agricultural productivity continues to rise and as China's economy shifts away from a labor-intensive model, rural unemployment is expected to increase further. New job opportunities in China's emerging green sectors will help relieve the social burden of unemployment in more traditional economic sectors.

China's green economy plans are focused in three broad target areas: boosting the share of renewable energy in the country's energy supply; preserving and enhancing the country's natural assets, particularly forests; and embracing new technologies to reduce the environmental impacts of traditionally "dirty" sectors.[26] But greening can and should occur in all sectors of the economy. UNEP's 2010 *Green Economy Report*, for example, focuses on initiatives being taken worldwide in 11 sectors: agriculture, buildings, cities, energy, fisheries, forests, manufacturing, tourism, transport, waste, and water.[27]

The following analysis explores greening activities in three leading sectors of China's economy—energy, transportation, and forestry—covering activities in each of the three target areas. These sectors are chosen both for their overall importance and because they offer the most data on environmentally sustainable economic development in China. The report sheds light on the current scale of investment and employment in these sectors and also offers estimates of potentials for 2020.* In doing so, it provides the clearest picture to date of the implications of China's green economy transition both for the world's most populous country and for the rest of the planet.

* Due to data availability, this report relies on a mix of methodologies to derive green jobs estimates for China. Input-output models, which seek to capture direct and indirect employment and to estimate net employment impacts, are used to the extent possible, based on the 2007 China Input-Output Table. For sectors not clearly specified in the table, the report relies on industry surveys or expert interviews. Calculations are generally based on a key underlying assumption, such as reaching a given level of spending or achieving a specific policy goal (for example, generating a certain share of the energy supply from renewable sources by a target year). The methodologies for each sectoral analysis are clarified in the endnotes as necessary.

Greening the Energy Supply

China's energy sector is heavily dependent on coal, which emits more carbon dioxide into the atmosphere per unit of energy released than any other energy source. The country has vast coal reserves and relies on this fossil fuel for roughly 75 percent of its energy production and 68 percent of its energy consumption—much higher shares than in the rest of the world.[1] Coal-fired power generation accounted for at least 80 percent of the nation's total electricity supply from 2002–08.[2]

Not surprisingly, coal also is responsible for roughly 80 percent of China's carbon dioxide emissions, with more than half of this coming from thermal power generation.[3] In 2006, China passed the United States to become the world's largest emitter of industrial CO_2.[4] Coal is also an important contributor to air pollution, acid rain, and human health problems nationwide.

In 2009, China passed the United States to become the world's largest energy consumer, according to the International Energy Agency.[5] Although China aims to increase the share of renewable energy in its energy mix to 15 percent by 2020, projections indicate that the country's total energy consumption will continue to rise and that coal will remain dominant. For instance, more than 60 percent of China's electricity in 2020 is still expected to come from coal-fired power plants.[6] (See Figure 1.)

Increasing the share of renewable energy sources—particularly wind and solar power—would contribute significantly to emissions reductions and play a vital role in greening China's energy supply. According to the draft *Development Plan for Emerging New Energy Industry*, China aims to invest some 5 trillion yuan ($770 billion) in new energy-related sectors between 2011 and 2020.[7] Of this, some 2–3 trillion yuan ($308–462 billion) will be investments in renewable energy (excluding hydropower).[8]

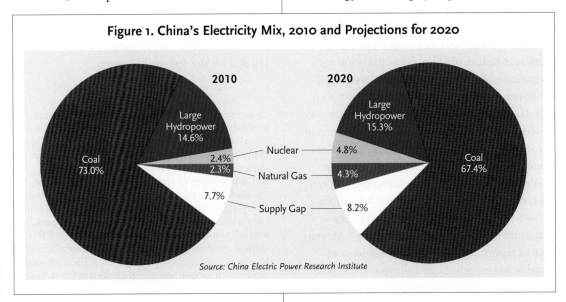

Figure 1. China's Electricity Mix, 2010 and Projections for 2020

2010
Large Hydropower 14.6%
Coal 73.0%
Nuclear — 2.4%
Natural Gas — 2.3%
Supply Gap — 7.7%

2020
Large Hydropower 15.3%
Coal 67.4%
Nuclear — 4.8%
Natural Gas — 4.3%
Supply Gap — 8.2%

Source: China Electric Power Research Institute

A wide variety of approaches are available for greening the energy supply, including the use of technologies such as carbon capture and storage (CCS) to transform existing fossil fuel power generation. Due to data availability, however, this report focuses on economic and employment prospects in three renewable energy sectors that are advancing rapidly in China: solar hot water, solar photovoltaics, and wind power.

Solar Hot Water

In a little over a decade, China has made unprecedented achievements in solar water heating. Solar hot water accounted for half of the country's total renewable energy use of 50 million tons of coal equivalent (tce) in 2008, excluding large hydropower and traditional biomass.[9] That year, Chinese companies manufactured 31 million square meters of solar water heaters, accounting for 76 percent of global production.[10]

In 2009, China added another 42 million square meters of solar hot water, for a total of 177 million square meters installed.[11] (See Figure 2.) This surpassed the national goal of 150 million square meters by 2010 (as outlined in the *Medium-and-Long Term Development Plan for Renewable Energy*) and represented more than 80 percent of the world total.[12]

Solar water heating, together with other solar thermal applications such as solar cookstoves and solar houses, is expected to replace more than 50 million tce of China's energy use annually.[13] And there is significant potential for further growth. Estimates suggest that if just 20 percent of the country's roof area were devoted to solar water heating systems, this would replace 340 million tons of coal, or 11.4 percent of China's 2008 coal consumption.[14]

China is by far the world's leading manufacturer of solar water heaters, with domestic production capacity topping 40 million square meters in 2009.[15] As of 2010, more than 2,000 manufacturers of these systems were operating at scale.[16] China is positioning itself as the technology leader in this area. Annual production of Chinese-developed vacuum-tube solar heating systems, among the most advanced in the world, now exceeds 16 million square meters.[17] These systems are being used widely domesti-

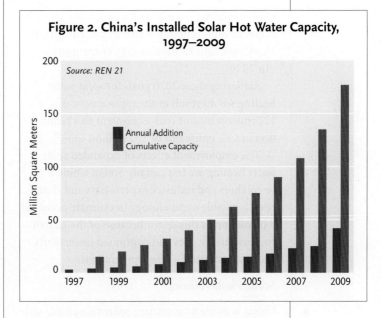

Figure 2. China's Installed Solar Hot Water Capacity, 1997–2009

Source: REN 21

- Annual Addition
- Cumulative Capacity

cally and are also exported to Asia, Europe, and Africa. Chinese manufacturers boast a remarkable 90 percent of the global market for these products.[18]

Although comprehensive data on solar hot water in China are lacking,* the 2010 *Research Report on Development of China's Solar Thermal Industry* provides projections for growth of the solar thermal sector to 2020.[19] According to the report's medium scenario:

- Annual production of solar water heaters will reach 135 million square meters in 2015 and 273 million square meters in 2020;
- Annual production of solar water heaters will reach a nominal value of 180 billion yuan ($28 billion) by 2015 and 380 billion yuan ($58 billion) by 2020;
- Total installation of solar water heaters will reach 400 million square meters in 2015 and 800 million square meters in 2020;
- Annual exports of solar water heaters will reach $500 million by 2015 and $1 billion by 2020; and

---

* Rapid development of the solar heating industry and the dispersive nature of installation and maintenance services have prevented the creation of a sectorwide dataset for solar hot water in China. Existing industry surveys do not provide details on the methodology and datasets used, and industrial associations and energy research institutes offer varying visions for future development. Because the industry is primarily market-oriented, the Chinese government does not provide a detailed development plan as it does for wind and solar photovoltaic.

• Solar thermal overall will account for 16 percent of total renewable energy consumption and 2 percent of total energy consumption in 2020.

Achieving these 2020 goals for solar water heating would result in the replacement of some 122 million tons of coal, equivalent to a reduction in CO_2 emissions of 262 million tons.[20]

The employment effects of expanded solar water heating are less certain. So far, Chinese researchers and industry experts have not developed a reliable methodology to estimate potential job creation in this sector because of the lack of comprehensive data and continued uncertainty about the industry's development path.

Solar Photovoltaics

China is home to abundant solar resources, with an annual usable capacity equivalent to 2.4 trillion tce.[21] The most promising resources are located in the country's northwest, including in Xizang, Qinghai, Xinjiang, Gansu, and Ningxia provinces, and Inner Mongolia.[22] (See Figure 3.) Given the scale of this solar capital, there is significant potential for solar power to become an important part of China's energy mix.

Generally speaking, there are two kinds of solar power-generation technologies: solar photovoltaic (PV) and solar thermal. Because the latter is not yet commercialized in China and

Figure 3. Map of Solar Radiation Intensity in China

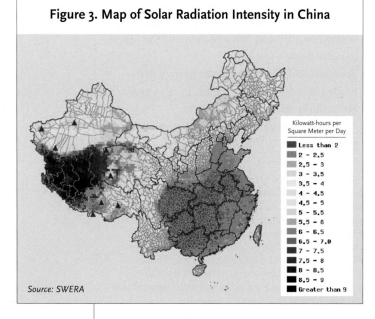

Source: SWERA

remains mostly at the demonstration stage, this report focuses on solar PV manufacturing and power generation activities.

PV Manufacturing

Since 2003, China's solar photovoltaic manufacturing industry has experienced rapid growth. Domestic solar cell production reached 1.2 gigawatts (GW) in 2006, and in 2008 China overtook both Japan and Europe to become the largest PV manufacturer worldwide.[23] With improvements in technology and newly added capacity for producing solar silicon materials, China is starting to develop a comprehensive PV industry.[24] By June 2008, the country was home to nearly 700 PV manufacturing companies, of which roughly 40 were focused on polysilicon materials, 70 on silicon ingots, 40 on solar batteries, and more than 500 on PV components and other applications.[25] In 2010, four out of the global top 10 solar PV cell manufacturers were Chinese companies.[26]

According to industry reports, China's PV manufacturing industry had cumulative sales of 88 billion yuan ($13.5 billion) and employed some 83,000 workers in 2007—up sharply from only 13 billion yuan ($2 billion) and 13,800 workers in 2005.[27] (See Table 1.) Although more recent data are not available, it can be assumed that both sales and employment have continued this strong growth.

Yet China's photovoltaic manufacturing industry faces great uncertainties, making it difficult to predict future prospects. Slow development of the country's solar power generation sector has stymied local demand for equipment and led to the creation of a manufacturing industry that is primarily export-oriented. Overcapacity is also a concern. Since 2009, the rapid growth in polysilicon manufacturing worldwide has led to a global glut in both the silicon supply and solar PV components. As a result, the PV market is characterized by redundant production capacity.

China alone had the capacity to produce more than 70,000 tons of polysilicon in 2010, enough to meet current global demand.[28] In August 2009, the government announced that it would establish new standards to regulate industry access and slow rampant development in photovoltaic manufacturing.[29] As more countries worldwide promote domestic renewable energy, however, China's export-oriented PV industry may face trade conflicts and other challenges that could significantly affect the sector's development.

PV Power Generation

PV power generation lags considerably behind PV manufacturing in China. Whereas the country's solar cell production increased more than 1,000 times between 1990 and 2007, the total installed PV power capacity increased only 39 times, starting from a very small base.[30] China's installed solar PV generation capacity reached 270 megawatts (MW) in 2009, with half of this total installed that year.[31] (See Figure 4.)

Based on the total installed capacity for 2006–10 and on projections for 2020 (see Table 2), it is possible to derive a rough estimate of job creation in China's PV power sector.[32] Our estimation shows that during the 11th Five-Year Period (2006–10), the sector generated an average of 2,700 direct jobs and 6,500 indirect jobs annually.* This is projected to increase to an average of 6,680 direct jobs and 16,370 indirect jobs annually between 2011 and 2020. Given the rapid growth in China's solar industry and potential upgrades in government projections, estimates for future green jobs could be much higher.

Wind Power

Since the mid-1990s, and especially during the 11th Five-Year Period (2006–10), China's wind energy sector has expanded dramatically. The country invested more than 300 billion yuan ($46 billion) in 378 new wind energy projects in 2010 alone.[33] By the end of the year, China's grid-connected installed wind power capacity reached 31 GW, second only to that of the United States.[34] If off-grid applications are

---

* Jobs here are defined as newly added one-year working opportunities. Due to limitations with the input-output method, estimates in this report capture only the employment opportunities created during the process of building solar PV power generation facilities. The operation and management share of potential employment is the subject of future studies. Direct jobs are jobs created directly in the target sector; indirect jobs are positions created in related sectors due to increased economic activity in the target sector.

Table 1. Employment and Sales in China's Solar Photovoltaic Manufacturing Industry, 2005–07

Industry Subsector	Employment (number of positions)		
	2005	2006	2007
Components	2,700	9,000	25,000
Silicon ingots/wafers	2,400	7,700	13,000
Batteries	1,500	4,800	11,000
Polysilicon	1,000	3,600	7,000
Systems engineering and marketing services	2,000	2,600	3,000
Special materials (glass, EVA, silver aluminum, etc.)	500	1,800	2,500
Balance components (inverter, battery, etc.)	500	1,000	1,500
Lighting, garden lights, consumer goods	3,000	8,500	1,500
Research and development	300	500	800
Total Employment	**13,800**	**39,500**	**82,800**
Total Industrial Sales (billion yuan)	**12.8**	**43.3**	**88.2**

Source: See Endnote 27 for this section.

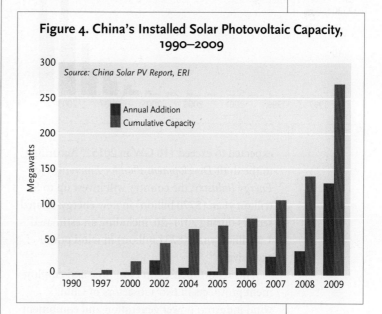

Figure 4. China's Installed Solar Photovoltaic Capacity, 1990–2009

Source: China Solar PV Report, ERI

included, this figure approaches 42 GW, making China the global leader in wind power development.[35] (See Figure 5.)

China's installed wind power capacity is

Table 2. China's Installed Solar Photovoltaic Capacity, Targets and Actual Capacity, 2006–20

	Annual Addition		Cumulative Installed Capacity	
Year	Target	Actual	Target	Actual
	megawatts			
2006	10	10	80	80
2007	20	26	100	106
2008	40	34	140	140
2009	160	130	300	270
2010	400	n/a	700	n/a
2020	—	—	1,800	—

Source: See Endnote 32 for this section.

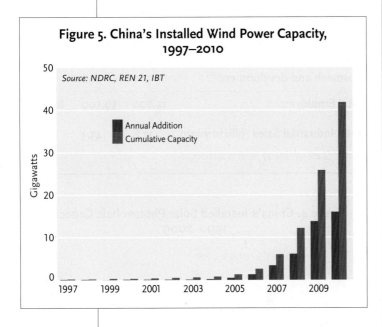

Figure 5. China's Installed Wind Power Capacity, 1997–2010

Source: NDRC, REN 21, IBT

Annual Addition
Cumulative Capacity

Wind Power Generation

Based on projections for China's wind power market, it is possible to estimate potential job creation in the sector. Industry data indicate that for every megawatt of installed wind power capacity, this requires the employment of 1.5–2 full-time workers (defined as operations personnel on wind farms).[39] Assuming that this ratio continues to hold as installed capacity expands, this means that China's wind power development during 2006–10 resulted in the creation of some 61,000 to 81,400 full-time positions.[40] (See Table 3.) In 2010 alone, China's 16 GW of newly added wind power capacity created an estimated 24,000 to 32,000 new jobs. We estimate that there may be closer to 83,000 full-time employees working on China's 42 GW of installed wind turbines.

To meet its 2020 goal for wind power development of 120 GW, China will need to install an additional 78 GW of generation capacity between 2011 and 2020.[41] This could result in as many as 66,000 new jobs over this period, or an average of 6,600 jobs annually.[42] The actual number of green jobs in the sector could be far greater, however, because this estimate represents only operations personnel on wind farms and does not include potential installation workers needed. Moreover, at the current pace of wind development, China could achieve much greater installed capacity by 2020.[43]

Using the available multipliers for indirect employment, it can be estimated that China's wind power development generated an average of 32,000 indirect jobs annually between 2006 and 2010.[44] The addition of 78 GW of capacity between 2011 and 2020 would generate an average of 30,000 indirect jobs annually in related sectors during this period.

Wind Turbine Manufacturing

China's wind turbine manufacturing sector offers significant potential for green jobs as well. In 2007, the average per-kilowatt price for a wind turbine in China was 6,000–7,000 yuan ($924–1,078).[45] With increasing economies of scale, the price dropped to roughly 4,000 yuan ($616) in 2008 and even lower in 2010.[46] Assuming an average turbine price of 6,500 yuan in 2006–07, 4,000 yuan in 2008–10, and 3,500 yuan in 2011–20, it is possible to estimate the annual investment needs

expected to exceed 110 GW in 2015.[36] According to the draft *Development Plan for Emerging New Energy Industry*, the country will invest up to 5 trillion yuan ($770 billion) in new energy-related sectors during 2011–20, including an estimated 1.5 trillion yuan ($231 billion) in wind power exclusively.[37]

This report focuses on economic and employment prospects in two subsectors of China's wind industry: power generation and equipment manufacturing.[38] Additional subsectors, such as research and development (R&D), consulting, and other technical services, are not covered due to limited data availability.

Table 3. Employment in China's Wind Power Industry, 2006–10

Year	Annual Addition to Installed Capacity	Employment
	gigawatts	positions created
2006	1.34	2,000–2,700
2007	3.4	5,200–6,900
2008	6.1	9,200–12,200
2009	13.8	20,700–27,600
2010	16.0	24,000–32,000
Total (2006–10)	**40.7**	**61,000–81,400**

Source: See Endnote 40 for this section.

and job creation in the country's wind turbine industry.[47] (See Table 4.)

Assuming that there was no significant change in China's economic infrastructure, and assuming that the share of wind turbines produced domestically reached the government-mandated level of 80 percent, the wind equipment manufacturing sector generated an estimated 50,000 direct jobs in 2010. For the 2006–10 period, this total rises to 126,200 jobs. Due to the lack of reliable data on Chinese turbine exports, however, this green jobs estimate does not capture the full employment effect of China's wind manufacturing industry.

For the 2011–20 period, based on the addition of 78 GW of wind capacity and assuming that 80 percent of equipment is produced domestically, an estimated 219 billion yuan will need to be invested in China's turbine manufacturing sector. This would lead to an average of 21,000 new jobs created annually during this period.

Using the available indirect employment multipliers, it can be estimated that China's turbine manufacturing sector generated an average of 67,000 indirect jobs annually between 2006 and 2010. Meeting the equipment demands of an additional 78 GW of capacity by 2020 would require adding an average of 56,000 jobs annually to turbine manufacturing-related sectors.

In total, China's wind power industry—both the power generation and turbine manufacturing sectors—created an average of 40,000 direct green jobs annually between 2006 and 2010. Even factoring in increased productivity, China's wind power development between 2011 and 2020 will continue to generate an estimated 34,000 green jobs annually on average. Although not all of the indirect jobs associated with the wind power industry can be considered green jobs, the sheer scale of indirect employment—averaging 1 million jobs annually for 2006–10 and 86,000 jobs annually for 2011–20—suggests that China's massive wind development plans make an important contribution to the overall economy.

Table 4. China's Wind Turbine Manufacturing and Job Creation, 2006–10

Year	Newly Installed Turbine Capacity	Share of Turbines Domestically Produced	Turbine Capacity Domestically Produced*	Investment in Turbine Production	Direct Employment
	gigawatts	percent	gigawatts	billion yuan	jobs created
2006	1.3	45	0.6	3.8	3,660
2007	3.3	58	1.9	12.4	12,010
2008	6.2	76	4.7	18.6	18,050
2009	13.8	80	11.0	44.2	42,850
2010	16.0	80	12.8	51.2	49,670
Total (2006–10)					**126,240**

Because some of China's annual added turbine capacity is imported equipment, the table breaks out the portion of capacity produced only by domestic manufacturers.

Source: See Endnote 47 for this section.

Greening Transportation

China's transportation sector, like its energy sector, is undergoing a transformation. As the average wealth of Chinese citizens increases, the former "kingdom of bicycles" is experiencing a swell of motorization. In 2009, China overtook the United States to become the world's largest automotive market, home to some 170 million vehicles.[1] The transportation sector now accounts for just over one-tenth of China's total primary energy consumption, although this remains well below the U.S. transportation sector's share of 28 percent.[2] As its vehicle volume continues to grow, China's energy consumption from transportation will increase rapidly as well.

Traffic on Chang'an Avenue, Beijing.

China is expected to add as many as 220 million new vehicles between now and 2020.[3] Yet there is a green lining to this increasing mobility. The government plans to invest trillions of dollars between now and 2020 to make the transportation sector more environmentally sustainable, and it is adopting low-pollution strategies to both meet rising vehicle demand and improve public transport.

China's rising interest in green transportation is in large part a response to the environmental and social problems associated with the country's rapid transition to a "car-and-truck" economy. Air pollution routinely cloaks many Chinese cities, and congestion of roads and highways is becoming a painful fact of life. The most extreme illustration of this growing headache was a nearly two-week traffic jam that occurred north of Beijing in August 2010.[4]

Notably, this traffic jam was caused in part by the country's growing energy needs. In 2009, after the Chinese government began implementing coal industry reforms in Shanxi province, China's largest coal production base, Inner Mongolia became the alternative major coal supplier. This geographical shift led to a dramatic increase in heavy truck traffic along highways connecting Inner Mongolia to Beijing, which were not projected to accommodate such an increase in fleet volume until 2035.[5]

Although data on green transportation in China are sparse, various analyses explore elements of this transition. Intercity and urban rail, for example, have attracted tremendous investment in China and can be considered "green" approaches when compared to fossil fuel-intensive road and air transport. Between 2005 and 2008, investment in China's intercity and urban rail industry jumped from 170 billion yuan ($26 billion) to more than 530 billion yuan ($82 billion).[6] During that same period, the "green" share of China's overall transportation investment increased from 16.5 percent to 28 percent.[7]

Data on employment in China's green transportation sector are similarly sparse, although estimates have been derived for certain subsectors. Assuming that intercity rail and urban public transport (including urban rail as well as public buses) are green transportation options, then these sectors supported as many as 2.9 million green jobs in 2009, accounting for 62 percent of total transport employment, according to China's *2010 Statistical Yearbook*.[8]

This report focuses on economic and employment prospects in three green transportation subsectors: China's alternative-fuel vehicle industry (the development of hybrid cars and electric cars); the high-speed rail sector; and urban rail in Beijing.

Alternative Fuel Vehicles

China is experiencing a boom in private vehicle ownership. On average, the country's vehicle fleet increased 14.5 percent annually between 2000 and 2009.[9] The number of private cars alone more than doubled between 2005 and 2008.[10] According to the China Association of Automobile Manufacturers, the country produced 18.3 million vehicles in 2010, and 18.1 million vehicles were sold that year.[11] As elsewhere, almost all cars in China run on gasoline.

Despite its relative newness, the Chinese market for alternatively fueled vehicles is expanding rapidly. In January 2009, four government bodies[*] jointly initiated the "Ten Cities, One Thousand Vehicles" project to promote fuel-efficient and alternative-fuel vehicles. The goal is to deploy an average of 1,000 hybrid and/or electric vehicles for public service use in each of 10 pilot cities annually between 2009 and 2012.[12] By mid-2010, China was home to an estimated 5,000 alternative-fuel vehicles, with a combined distance of just over 81 million kilometers traveled.[13]

The Chinese government aims to achieve a 10-percent market share for so-called "new-energy vehicles"—including hybrid-electric,

---

* The Ministry of Science and Technology (MOST), Ministry of Finance, National Development and Reform Commission (NDRC), and Ministry of Industry and Information Technology (MIIT).

electric, and fuel-cell vehicles—by 2012. To encourage rapid uptake, in 2009 and 2010 the government expanded the promotion of alternative-fuel vehicles to private buyers and released a series of financial incentives for their purchase, including a subsidy cap of 60,000 yuan ($9,200) per vehicle.[14] As of October 2010, an estimated 8.5 billion yuan ($1.3 billion) had been invested in China's electric vehicle industry through capital markets.[15]

Brochure cover for the Benni Mini electric car.

Based on China's total investment in developing and producing new energy vehicles, it is possible to calculate potential job creation in this sector during the 2011–20 period.[16] If the government prioritizes the development of alternative-fuel vehicles, then cumulative production of hybrid and electric vehicles could reach 16.7 million (15 percent of total vehicle production), or an average of 1.67 million vehicles annually. This would lead to the creation of roughly 1.2 million green jobs annually in this sector on average. Under a less rosy development scenario, however, China's alternative fuel vehicle industry would generate an average of only 640,000 jobs annually between 2011 and 2020.

High-Speed Rail

China's first high-speed rail line was established only in 2004, yet the country has already become the global leader in high-speed rail (HSR) development. By the end of 2010, China was home to 17 HSR lines with a total operational length of some 8,400 kilometers, making it the most extensive HSR network in the world.[17] According to the country's *Long-Term Railway Network Plan*, which was updated in 2008, China aims to have 18,000 kilometers of HSR by 2020.[18]

© Nikada

The Shanghai Transrapid maglev train leaving the station.

To reach this goal, China will need to build another 10,000 kilometers of HSR lines over the coming decade. Based on the calculation that building 1 kilometer of HSR costs roughly 112 million yuan ($17.3 million), this brings the total investment needed for the remaining lines to 1.11 trillion yuan ($171 billion).[19] Applying employment coefficients to these investment figures translates into an average of 230,000 direct and 400,000 indirect jobs created annually during the 2011–20 period, or a total of 630,000 jobs annually.[20]

Urban Rail

In 2006, China's urban rail network—defined here as metro and light rail systems*—transported 1.8 billion passengers, twice as many as in 2001.[21] During this same period, rail's share

---

* Other urban rail formats, such as trams and those based on magnetic levitation ("maglevs"), are not discussed in this report due to their low prevalence in China. Only two commercialized maglev lines exist in China, in Shanghai and Beijing, and trams are found only in a few medium-sized cities, including Dalian, Changchun, and Anshan.

of urban passenger transport increased from 2.4 percent to 3.9 percent.[22] Since then, urban rail has continued to expand.

As of 2007, 10 Chinese municipalities boasted urban rail systems, with a total of 30 lines in operation.[23] By 2010, this total had increased to 37 lines, with a combined length of 1,130 kilometers.[24] Shanghai and Beijing have the longest urban rail networks by far, spanning 420 kilometers and 330 kilometers respectively in 2010.[25] Shanghai's metro, which added lines during the 2010 World Expo, has overtaken London's to become the world's most extensive subway network.[26]

During the 10th Five-Year Period (2001–05), China invested 200 billion yuan ($31 billion) in urban rail construction.[27] The country deployed more than 400 kilometers of urban rail, of which 293 kilometers are metro lines.[28] Twenty-five of China's 48 cities with more than 1 million residents are planning a combined total of 5,000 kilometers of urban rail systems, at an estimated investment cost exceeding 800 billion yuan ($123 billion).[29]

Although data limitations make it difficult to estimate the employment effect of China's urban rail sector, specific analysis of urban rail in Beijing allows for broader insight into these green jobs potentials.[30]

Beijing's municipal government has stepped up its urban rail ambitions in recent years. Current targets include completion of 660 kilometers of lines by 2015, at a total investment of 500 billion yuan ($77 billion), and construction of another 340 kilometers of lines during 2016–20, at a total investment of 445 billion yuan ($69 billion).[31] These investment projections can be used to estimate the future employment effects of Beijing's urban rail development plan.[32] (See Table 5.)

For the period from 2011 through 2015, investment in Beijing's urban rail systems could create an average of 164,000 direct jobs and close to 300,000 indirect jobs annually. Further development of urban rail from 2016 through 2020 to achieve the municipal government's target could create an average of 146,000 direct jobs and 266,300 indirect jobs annually. Overall, from 2011 through 2020, development of urban rail in Beijing could bring more than 437,000 jobs each year.

These trends in China's transportation sector—for alternative-fuel vehicles, high-speed rail, and urban rail—suggest that the nation's green development strategy is not only compatible with economic growth, but can serve as a powerful economic driver. The rest of the world may face difficulties trying to match China's tremendous investment in green transportation. The Chinese example only strengthens the case for a global green transition and can boost worldwide confidence about the benefits of green growth in both developing and developed countries.

Table 5. Job Creation Potentials in Beijing's Urban Rail Transit, 2011–20

	Direct Employment	Indirect Employment	Total Employment
		number of positions	
2011–15	820,200	1,496,100	2,316,300
2016–20	730,000	1,331,500	2,061,500
Total (2011–20)	**1,550,200**	**2,827,600**	**4,377,800**

Source: See Endnote 32 for this section.

Greening the Forestry Sector

orests serve as the Earth's largest terrestrial carbon reservoir and play an important role in maintaining the carbon balance through carbon sequestration and oxygen release. Managing forest ecosystems is also vital to protecting biodiversity and ecosystem health. In China, forests are home to more than 1,800 species of wild animals, more than 2,000 tree species, and more than 6,000 species of bushes, hundreds of which are found only in China.[1]

From an economic perspective, China's forestry sector includes various subsectors such as cultivation, planting, and management; logging and timber transport; processing and manufacturing of forest products; and cultivation of flowers and bamboos. Newer subsectors in recent decades include forest tourism, forest ecosystem management, and forest bio-industry.

China's forestry sector saw rapid expansion during the period from 2006 through 2010, outpacing GDP with an average annual growth rate of 18.3 percent.[2] (See Figure 6.) Assuming similar growth in the future, China's forestry sector could be worth as much as 4.1 trillion yuan ($632 billion) in 2015 and 8 trillion yuan ($1.2 trillion) in 2020.[3] More than half of this annual revenue, however, comes from timber-related activities and cannot be considered part of the green economy. Due to data limitations, this report focuses on economic and employment prospects in three non-timber forestry subsectors: forestation, forest management, and forest tourism.

Forestation

Relative to the global average, China does not have abundant forest resources. According to the State Forestry Administration (SFA), forest

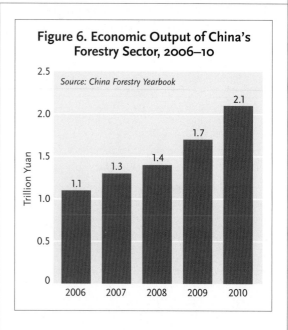

Figure 6. Economic Output of China's Forestry Sector, 2006–10

Source: China Forestry Yearbook

coverage nationwide in 2009 was only 20.4 percent—roughly two-thirds the worldwide average and lagging behind 138 other countries.[4] China's per capita forest area and forest reserve are one-fourth and one-seventh the global average, respectively.

Considering that China's forest coverage was as low as 8.6 percent in 1948, however, it is apparent that government-led forestation efforts—planting activities undertaken to create forest area—have been effective.[5] Of 195 million hectares of forest in China, some 62 million were planted, the largest such area worldwide.[6] Although the annual forestation area has fluctuated over the past half-century, it generally ranges between 3 and 6 million hectares.[7] (See Figure 7.)

Government-led forestation efforts in China include both afforestation (the establishment of forest where there was none before) and reforestation (the establishment of forest in areas where

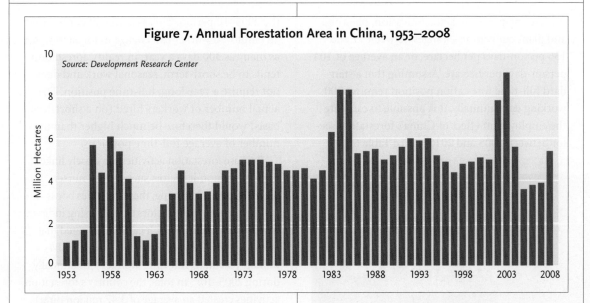

Figure 7. Annual Forestation Area in China, 1953–2008

Source: Development Research Center

trees or forest have been removed*). A major SFA initiative is the Six Key Forestry Projects, which includes programs to protect natural forest resources; restore agricultural lands to forest; control the sources of sandstorms in Beijing and Tianjin; create shelter forests in various regions; protect wildlife and establish nature reserves; and cultivate fast-growing and high-yield forests in barren areas. Between 1999 and 2008, these projects added some 52 million hectares of forest area, increasing China's forest coverage by more than 30 percent.[8] In 2009, they added another 4.6 million hectares of forest area, or nearly three-quarters of the total forestation that year.[9]

In addition, the government has initiated a national campaign to encourage voluntary tree-planting. Since 1979, March 12 has been designated as National Arbor Day, when citizens ranging from high-ranking members of the Communist Party to elementary school students participate in collective tree-planting activities. Between 1982 and 2009, more than 56 billion trees were planted through this campaign.[10]

China's forestation efforts have resulted in significant environmental benefits. Data from the National Climate Change Program indicate that forestation activities, including both national

programs and voluntary tree-planting by individuals, absorbed as much as 3.1 billion tons of carbon dioxide between 1980 and 2005.[11] Meanwhile, the pace of desertification has slowed from an average annual expansion of 3,500 cubic kilometers in the late 1990s to less than 1,300 cubic kilometers in 2010.[12]

By the end of 2010, China had designated more than 122 million hectares, about 2.7 percent of its territory, as nature reserves.[13] The country now boasts more than 2,150 forest parks, spanning 16 million hectares nationwide, which play a crucial role in protecting biodiversity.[14] More than 95 million hectares of natural forest were considered "protected" in 2010, helping to decrease forest resource usage by 426 million cubic meters in total.[15]

In total, China's forests provide an estimated 10 trillion yuan ($1.54 trillion) in ecosystem services each year.[16] This includes conserving some 500 billion cubic meters of fresh water, solidifying more than 7 billion tons of soil, preserving some 364 million tons of nutrients; absorbing 32 million tons of air pollutants, and keeping down up to 5 billion tons of dust.[17] In 2008, China's forestation activities generated an economic output of 48 billion yuan ($7.4 billion), representing 3.3 percent of the forestry economy.[18]

As a labor-intensive activity, forestation can significantly increase employment, especially in rural areas. According to the SFA, the typical working time required for forestation—includ-

---

* In principle, reforestation can be done either naturally (by natural seeding, coppice, or root suckers) or artificially (by direct seeding or planting). This report covers only the artificial share of reforestation activities.

ing land preparation, land cultivation, planting, and plant cultivation—ranges between 71 and 136 person-days per hectare, or an average of 104 person-days per hectare. Assuming that a standard full-time forestation position requires 300 working days annually, it is possible to estimate the employment effect of China's forestation sector between 2005 and 2010.[20] (See Table 6.)

Encroaching desert near the western end of the Great Wall at Jiayuguan, Gansu province.

Table 6. Job Creation from Forestation Activities in China, 2005–08

Year	Annual Forestation Area	Working Days Needed	Direct Job Creation
	million hectares	million	million year-long positions
2005	3.6	377	1.3
2006	3.8	397	1.3
2007	3.9	405	1.4
2008	5.4	554	1.9
2009	6.3	648	2.2
2010	5.3	549	1.8

Source: See Endnote 20 for this section.

Based on this analysis, it can be estimated that the forestation sector employed as many as 1.8 million full-time workers in 2010 alone, or an average of 1.6 million workers annually during the 2005–10 period. This assumes, of course, that an employed worker can engage in forestation for as many as 300 days a year; in reality, forestation tends to be short-term, seasonal work and does not require a year-long, full-time position. The actual number of workers hired (on a short-term basis) would therefore be much higher than the number of average full-time positions.

Because forestation activities are closely linked to other economic sectors such as seed nurseries and technical training, these activities boost employment in these sectors as well. Using indirect employment multipliers, it can be estimated that forestation in China created an average of 1.84 million year-long, full-time indirect jobs annually during 2005–10.[21] In total, the country's forestation activities created an average of 3.47 million direct and indirect jobs annually during this period.

The prospects for continued green jobs creation from forestation are high. At the United Nations climate change conference in Copenhagen, Denmark, in 2009, President Hu Jintao stated that an important way for China to mitigate the effects of climate change is to "increase forest coverage by 40 million hectares and forest reserves by 1.3 billion cubic meters [from the 2005 level] by 2020."[22] Assuming that forestation continues to account for 3.3 percent of the forestry sector's economic output, these activities could be worth 130 billion yuan ($20 billion) by 2015 and 270 billion yuan ($42 billion) by 2020.

According to our estimation, achieving these goals for the coming decade would require a total of 1.56 billion working days, providing full-time employment for an average of 520,000 forestation workers annually between 2011 and 2020.[23] In addition, forestation activities could create an average of 590,000 indirect jobs annually in related sectors during this period. Overall, China's forestation activities could offer as many as 1.1 million direct and indirect jobs annually during 2011–20. This employment potential should not be interpreted as "new jobs," however, due to the short-term nature of forestation work.

Forest Management

After forestation takes place, careful management is generally needed to help preserve and maintain this valuable green capital. In China, most forest management duties are undertaken by forest rangers who are responsible for tasks such as monitoring and preventing forest fires, preventing illegal logging and wildlife hunting, and identifying forest pests.

Specific data on China's forest management subsector are not available; however, official Chinese statistics include these activities under the general category of "public forestry management and related services," which was valued at 10.6 billion yuan ($1.6 billion) in 2008.[24] Although forest management accounts for only a small share of China's forestry economy, as with forestation it has significant environmental value and is therefore a crucial sector of the green economy.

Based on China's annual forestation area and the SFA's guideline that each full-time forest manager should oversee no more than 150 hectares of forest per year, it is possible to estimate direct job creation from forest management in recent years.[25] In total, more than 188,000 full-time forest management jobs were created during the 2005–10 period, including some 35,000 positions in 2010 alone.[26] (See Table 7.) This estimate captures only the employment effects of newly added forest area, due to the lack of relevant data for existing forests. If all forest area were included, the actual number of forest management jobs in China would be much higher.

Based on the indirect employment multiplier, each direct job in China's forest management sector would create a further 1.48 jobs in related sectors.[27] This results in more than 52,000 indirect jobs created in 2010, or an average of 46,000 jobs created annually from 2005 through 2010.

Looking ahead, the estimated forestation area needed to achieve the government's 2020 goal is 18.3 million hectares.[28] Managing this newly added forest area during 2011–20 would require some 1.2 million employees. Assuming 3 percent annual growth in productivity on average, direct job creation would drop to 1.04 million. Correspondingly, these new forest management jobs would help bring 1.5–1.8 million new jobs in related sectors during the 2011–20 period.

Forest Tourism

A third significant "green" sector in China is forest tourism, defined as tourism activities under-

Table 7. Job Creation from Forest Management in China, 2005–10

Year	Annually Added Forest Area	Direct Job Creation
	million hectares	number of full-time positions*
2005	3.6	24,251
2006	3.8	25,592
2007	3.9	26,051
2008	5.4	35,699
2009	6.3	41,749
2010	5.3	35,333
Total	**28.3**	**188,675**

* Forest management jobs are considered long-term positions. Because these jobs increase as the forested area expands, job creation here refers to the net increment.

Source: See Endnote 26 for this section.

taken to appreciate forest scenic resources. China's forest tourism involves mainly the establishment of forest recreation areas, such as forest parks, nature reserves, scenic spots, botanical gardens, and state-operated forest farms, as well as the development of associated resources. Due to limited data availability, this report focuses on the economic and employment prospects related to forest parks, which account for 70–80 percent of forest tourism activities.[29] Consequently, any

A forest park in Shanghai.

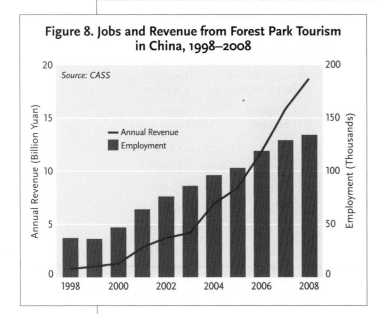

Figure 8. Jobs and Revenue from Forest Park Tourism in China, 1998–2008

Source: CASS

tation, infrastructure, forest cultivation, water conservation, religion, and the service and leisure industries. Development of this industrial chain will speed job creation in related sectors, especially in newer areas such as forest healthcare (using forest resources to improve people's health), forest industry investment, tourism employee training, and the leisure culture industry. Based on the indirect employment multiplier for China's tourism sector, which suggests that one job created in tourism will bring 1.55 jobs to related sectors, it can be calculated that forest tourism generated between 243,000 and 276,000 indirect jobs in 2010.[33]

Looking ahead, assuming that the annual revenue from forest park tourism will continue to increase by an average of 20 percent annually, by 2015 this sector could provide 273,000 direct jobs and generate 423,000 indirect jobs in related sectors. For 2020, these estimates would increase to 392,000 direct jobs and 607,000 indirect jobs, or a total of nearly 1 million green jobs.

By combining the job creation estimates in these three forestry-related subsectors—forestation, forest management, and forest tourism—it is possible to gain a rough sense of how many green jobs exist in China's forestry sector in a given year.* For 2010, for example, as many as 2 million newly created positions in the sector could be considered green jobs.

---

* Due to the different methodologies used to derive green jobs estimates in this report, it may not be appropriate to simply add these estimates together to derive an overall green jobs figure. However, such summation can be useful in providing a rough calculation of green jobs in a specific sector in a given year.

job creation estimates will be smaller than under the broader definition of forest tourism.

With more than 2,000 forest parks nationwide, China has great potential to expand this niche form of tourism. Between 1990 and 2008, the forestry department invested more than 1.1 billion yuan ($170 million) in forest park construction and maintenance, according to *China's Forestry Yearbook*.[30] In 2008, the sector generated nearly 19 billion yuan ($2.9 billion) in revenue and directly employed some 140,000 full-time workers.[31] (See Figure 8.) Although data for more recent years are not available, estimates suggest that in 2010, revenue totaled 27–29.3 billion yuan ($4.2–4.5 billion) and the sector generated some 178,000 direct jobs.[32]

Forest tourism has strong linkages with other economic sectors including business, transpor-

Accelerating China's Green Transition

Based on the analysis provided above, it can be stated with confidence that the three sectors highlighted in this report—energy, transportation, and forestry—could provide at least 4.5 million green jobs in 2020. If these sectors continue their rapid expansion, and if similar estimates could be obtained for other emerging green sectors in China, it would be evident that the economy-wide potential for green jobs is enormous.

Greening initiatives in these leading economic sectors indicate that the Chinese government is making great strides in shifting the country's economic development to a more sustainable path. As a largely top-down political system, China has set goals for nearly every aspect of sustainable development over the coming decade. With tremendous investment already approved and additional support policies being planned, the country has established a long-term green vision and will almost certainly meet or surpass its ambitious green economy goals.

Yet a green vision alone is not enough; attention also needs to be paid to the actual steps being taken to achieve those goals. Ultimately, it is not the green development policies and plans, but rather their effective implementation, that will make a measurable difference for China's environment and for human well-being. Indeed, one of the greatest lessons to be learned from the early days of China's green transition is that building a sustainable future requires using approaches and processes that are sustainable in practice as well.

Due largely to inefficient implementation, several key green development measures in China have resulted in unintended economic or environmental costs. For example, although the country is now the world leader in installed wind power capacity, roughly one-third of this Chinese capacity has difficulty connecting to the grid, resulting in millions of dollars of investment loss.[1] The solar photovoltaic industry faces significant hurdles as well. China is the world's largest PV producer, yet domestic photovoltaic power remains in the early stages, and the country's export-oriented PV market has become overheated. Rapid growth in manufacturing and the lack of effective environmental enforcement have led to serious pollution problems.[2] China needs urgently to expedite domestic PV development if it hopes to further green its energy supply.

To avoid these and other costs, the Chinese government needs to enhance its administrative efficiency and to adopt new market-based approaches to create a supportive yet stable environment for nourishing the green economy. One challenge will be smoothing the rough edges in the relationships among different levels of government. In China, provincial and local governments are mandated to take the lead in implementing green development policies, yet their lack of coordination and their preference for actions that boost local GDP can impede efficient and effective implementation of national policy. Moreover, as China advances its economic and political reforms, the country has become less centralized than two decades ago, making relationships among the different levels of government increasingly complex.

Another significant barrier to China's green transition is the lack of basic research and statistical capacity. It is extremely difficult to find accurate, reliable data on economic and social trends in China, either because this has not been collected or because of problems with the existing statistical system. Expert estimates and projections often vary significantly, requiring careful scrutiny to determine their reliability and/or suitability to China's context.

This report represents the most thorough effort known to date to explore China's green economy and green jobs potentials. In the future, the availability of more comprehensive and more reliable data will allow for an expansion and deepening of this effort, enabling Chinese policymakers and other stakeholders to better understand the options that are available to them in pursuing an effective green transition.

Until then, the following recommendations can be used to help these and other actors facilitate the transition to a green economy in China:

1. **Enhance research and development (R&D) in key green technology areas.** Chinese "clean technology" industries maintain a significant competitive advantage in global manufacturing because of preferential government policies and low labor costs. But many Chinese industries lack the core or most-advanced technologies in their fields, meaning that they must either pay high licensing fees or import the necessary components at high cost. As the scale of Chinese clean tech expands, these industries will eventually need to develop their own R&D capacity to better position themselves in the global market. Enhancing R&D capacity will also bring related jobs. The Chinese government should continue to increase its R&D investment as well as create more reliable channels to help R&D projects grow into mature businesses.

2. **Emphasize the importance of sustainable policy implementation and build institutional mechanisms to ensure it.** Government decision makers need to understand that setting green development goals alone is not enough—that a successful shift to a green economy ultimately depends on how effective and efficient this transition process is. Policymakers should be more comprehensive in the design and planning of policy implementation, incorporating non-economic impacts such as environmental costs and the effects on human health. Green development policies should also lay out relevant support mechanisms to ensure that the policies are implemented in the most

sustainable manner possible. Mechanisms to ensure smooth and sustainable implementation need to be built into the policymaking process and determined before policies are finalized and released. Green development policies should also be subject to regulatory review to determine whether they meet sustainability standards, and greater transparency is needed in the policymaking process.

3. **Improve the role of market-based incentives and expedite maturity of China's market system more generally.** China has experimented with market-oriented reform since the late 1980s, but because the country's market system is not fully fledged, many market behaviors and actions remain subject to administrative decisions. Preferential policies provided the initial push for much of China's green economy, but as the scale and scope of green sectors expand, the quality of the transition will depend on a mature market system. The Chinese government needs to send a strong market signal to promote green development and ensure that the market mechanism carrying that signal is functioning well. In addition, governments at all levels need to nourish a fully functional labor market that is flexible enough to adjust to the rapid growth of emerging green sectors. A transitional labor market is needed to accommodate unemployed workers from traditional industries that are expected to be replaced with workers in newer, green industries.

4. **Enact a comprehensive capacity-building plan to better prepare for a full-speed green transition.** Data availability remains a major barrier to in-depth analysis of China's green economy. However, statistical challenges exist even in areas where strict evaluation systems have been established. For instance, although China has enacted a plan to assess the performance of provincial and local government officials in energy savings and emissions reduction, a recent report found that reliable data are not only unavailable but also difficult to improve upon because of the lack of expertise and training among local statistical staff.[3] China has committed internationally to reducing the carbon intensity of its economy 40–45 percent (from the 2005 level)

by 2020 and is holding provincial and local leaders accountable to achieve this goal. Consequently, the government needs to invest greater effort in improving the quality of its data collection and processing. More broadly, capacity building is needed in all green development areas, and the government should be coordinating this in an efficient manner.

5. **Initiate a national public education campaign to promote the concept and practice of green living.** The government has been the major promoter of nearly every significant social and economic reform in China in recent decades. The ease and quality of the green economy transition, however, will depend to a great extent on the support and behavior of the wider public. The government needs to design and implement a proper education campaign to increase public awareness of consumer behaviors that help bring about a green economy. Greater societal demand for green living would create a strong incentive for industries and businesses to be creative in fostering this shift. In addition to being large scale, the public education campaign needs to be of the highest quality possible. China is rife with examples of "greenwashing"—activities that create a public relations impression of environmental improvement—at all levels. These not only fail to meet reasonable standards of environmental sustainability but also distort the public's view of what a truly green economy is.[4]

6. **Elevate green development to a national strategy and develop a systematic plan for implementation.** In practice, the Chinese government considers many of the country's policies and actions to be greening efforts. But scaling up these efforts and creating effective synergies among them will require elevating green development to the level of national strategy. The government needs to issue specific policy measures that outline detailed workplans and support mechanisms for green development (including financing mechanisms) and to designate dedicated institutions to carry out the strategy. A sound, science-based green development strategy is needed to consolidate China's

Children are the future of China's green power.

Greenpeace/FU Xinghua

resources and talents and to help the country achieve a green economy in a sustainable manner. The process of forming such a strategy would allow for the evaluation of existing green development efforts, providing better guidance for expediting and improving the quality of China's green transition.

Already, China is taking the lead in green investment and has become a global leader in renewable energy development. As the government continues its efforts to improve energy efficiency and reduce greenhouse gas emissions, and as the Chinese public becomes more aware of the climate and environmental impacts associated with the country's "old" development path, the shift to a green economy is likely to gain momentum. Over the coming decades, the world will most likely witness China making ever greater strides toward evolving a green economy.

China's experience with green development will have a significant influence on efforts to establish green economies around the world. As the largest developing country and the world's second largest economy, China's achievement in a comprehensive, economy-wide national green transition would encourage countless other countries—developed and developing—to follow the challenging yet rewarding path toward true environmental sustainability.

Endnotes

China's Shift to a Green Economy

1. *Hold High the Great Banner of Socialism with Chinese Characteristics and Strive for New Victories in Building a Moderately Prosperous Society in All Respects*, Report to the Seventeenth National Congress of the Communist Party of China, 15 October 2007.

2. Hu Jintao, "Common Development and Prosperity," speech delivered at the CEO Summit of Asia-Pacific Economic Cooperation (APEC), Yokohama, Japan, 13 November 2010.

3. Li Keqiang, "The Chinese Government Attaches Great Importance to the Green Economy and Climate Change," keynote speech at the 2010 International Cooperative Conference on Green Economy and Climate Change, Beijing, 8 May 2010.

4. Beijing Center for Chinese Studies, "China's Environment," www.thebeijingcenter.org/chinagreen/about.

5. "China Overtakes Japan as World's Second-Biggest Economy," Bloomberg.com, 16 August 2010.

6. Zhang Jijuan et al. "Current Status and Characteristics of Urban Air Pollution in China" (in Chinese), *Sichuan Environment*, vol. 2, no. 3 (2006), at www.lw23.com/paper_23699191.

7. "Ten Most Polluted Places in the World" (in Chinese), http://grchina.com/gb/gbj/spot/spo06271.htm.

8. Ibid.

9. "China Overtakes U.S. in Greenhouse Gas Emissions," *New York Times*, 20 June 2007.

10. "China Should Expedite the Promotion of Carbon Capture and Storage Technology" (in Chinese), *Technology Daily*, 16 March 2010, at www.cas.cn/xw/zjsd/201003/t20100316_2798088.shtml.

11. National Bureau of Statistics, "2009 Statistical Communique for National Economy and Social Development" (in Chinese) (Beijing: 25 February 2010), at www.stats.gov.cn/tjgb/ndtjgb/qgndtjgb/t20100225_402622945.htm.

12. "Current Status of Water Pollution in China and the World" (in Chinese), *Bimonthly Review* (Beijing: 28 March 2006), at www.sxhn.cn/Article_Show.asp?articleid=6071.

13. Ibid.

14. "China's Water Crisis" (in Chinese), 24 March 2006, at www.china.com.cn/chinese/zhuanti/hjwj/1164436.htm.

15. Lu Ming, "Current Status of and Controlling Policies for China's Rural Environmental Pollution," *Agricultural Environment and Development*, Issue 3 (2009); Ju Guopeng et al., "Current Status of and Prevention Measures for China's Rural Environmental Pollution," *Science and Technology Information*, Issue 26 (2008).

16. "Current Status of China's Ecosystem" (in Chinese), http://loess.geodata.cn/html/kepu/docc/wenmingbrow.asp-id=1544&classid=60.html.

17. Ibid.

18. Ibid.

19. "How About the Current Biodiversity Status?" (in Chinese), *China Environmental News*, 3 June 2010, at http://env.people.com.cn/GB/11778117.html.

20. "Pollution Costs Equal 10% of China's GDP," *Shanghai Daily*, 6 June 2006.

21. "China Is Set to Lose 2% of GDP Cleaning Up Decades of Pollution," Bloomberg.com, 17 September 2010.

22. United Nations Environment Programme (UNEP), *Toward a Green Economy – A Synthesis for Policy Makers* (Nairobi: February 2011), p. 3.

23. National Bureau of Statistics, www.stats.gov.cn/tjsj/ndsj/.

24. "China's Unemployment Rate Hits 9.4%" (in Chinese), *China Economic Weekly*, January 2009, at http://business.sohu.com/20090105/n261565889.shtml.

25. "More than 100 Million Surplus Rural Labor Needs Jobs" (in Chinese), 10 September 2010, at www.chinanews.com/gn/2010/09-10/2526008.shtml.

26. UNEP, *Green Economy Report: A Preview* (Nairobi: May 2010), p. 3.

27. Ibid.

Greening the Energy Supply

1. National Bureau of Statistics, *China Statistical Yearbook 2009*, at www.stats.gov.cn/tjsj/ndsj/2009/indexch.htm.

2. "National Energy Administration Provides Energy Outlook" (in Chinese), at http://vnetcj.jrj.com.cn/2011/04/2218519805871-1.shtml.

3. "China Should Promote Carbon Dioxide Sequestration Technology" (in Chinese), at www.cas.cn/xw/zjsd/201003/t20100316_2798088.shtml.

Endnotes

4. "China Now Leads in Total Carbon Dioxide Emissions, Says Report," *EERE News*, http://apps1.eere.energy.gov/news/news_detail.cfm?news_id=11068.

5. "China Tops U.S. in Energy Use," *Wall Street Journal*, 18 July 2010.

6. Figure 1 from Hu Xuehao, *Specific Report on China's Medium and Long-term Energy Development Strategy* (Beijing: China Electric Power Research Institute, 2004). Note that this prediction, made in 2004, was overly optimistic about coal's diminished role in power generation in 2010. According to data from the National Development and Reform Commission (NDRC), coal's contribution to Chinese electricity production was still close to 80 percent in 2010, per NDRC, www.sdpc.gov.cn/jjxsfx/t20110211_394386.htm (in Chinese). The 2020 projection, however, is in line with other studies, such as www.sp.com.cn/zgdl/zgdlgk/200805/t20080515_103949.htm (in Chinese).

7. *Development Plan for Emerging New Energy Industry*, internal review draft. The official draft was scheduled for release during the first half of 2011.

8. Ibid.

9. Li Junfeng, "China Renewable Energy Development and Prospects in 2008" (Beijing: Chinese Renewable Energy Industries Association (CREIA), March 2009).

10. "A 2008-2009 Report on Jiangsu Province's Solar Water Heater Market" (in Chinese), *Xinhua Daily*, 10 June 2009.

11. Figure 2 from REN21, *Renewables 2010 Global Status Report* (Paris: 2010).

12. National goal is from NDRC, op. cit. note 6.

13. Li, op. cit. note 9

14. Chinese Academy of Engineering, *Strategic Research on China's Renewable Energy Development*, December 2008, at www.portworld.com/news/i90452/China_s_coal_consumption.

15. Ryan Rutkowski, "China Leads Solar Home Revolution," *Asia Times*, 29 October 2009.

16. Chinese Solar Industry Association, "How Many Solar Water Heater Producers in China?" (in Chinese), 1 July 2010, at www.cstif.cn/news/0907/01/11903f132Q33p.htm.

17. REN 21, *Recommendations for Improving the Effectiveness of Renewable Energy Policy in China* (Paris: October 2009).

18. Ibid.

19. China Association of Rural Energy Industry (CAREI), CREIA, and China Energy Conservation Association (CECA), *Research Report on Development of China Solar Thermal Industry: 2008-2010* (Beijing: August 2010) (in Chinese). If not specified otherwise, all remaining citations in this section come from this source.

20. Ibid.

21. "Solar PV Industry Prospects" (in Chinese), 29 September 2009, at http://yzh.smesd.gov.cn/Article_Show.asp?ArticleID=3900.

22. Figure 3 from Solar and Wind Energy Resource Assessment (SWERA), *Solar Energy in China*, available at www.geni.org/globalenergy/library/renewable-energy-resources/world/asia/solar-asia/solar-china.shtml.

23. "China Becomes the World's Second Largest Energy Producer" (in Chinese), *People's Daily*, 19 August 2008.

24. CCID Consulting, *Research Report on 2009-2010 China New Energy Industry Development*, provided by the Chinese Academy of Social Sciences.

25. "Industry Research Report on Major Listed Solar PV Companies, First Six Months of 2009" (in Chinese), at www.pesnet.net/study/market_589_73.html.

26. "Solarbuzz Reveals its Top 10 PV Cell Manufacturers of 2010," www.pv-tech.org/news/solarbuzz_reveals_its_top_10_pv_cell_manufacturers_of_2010.

27. Table 1 data from NDRC, Global Environment Facility, and World Bank, *China PV Industry Development Report (2004-2005)* and *China PV Industry Development (2006-2007)* (Beijing: China Renewable Energy Development Project).

28. Huatong Industrial Research Report, *2008-2009 China Solar PV Industry Development Report* (Beijing: 2010).

29. Ibid.

30. CCID Consulting, *New Energy Industry Development Report*, February 2010.

31. Ibid. Figure 4 from *China Solar PV Report* (Beijing: China Environmental Science Press, 2007) and on materials from the Energy Research Institute.

32. Annual goals in Table 2 are from *China Solar PV Report* (Beijing: China Environmental Science Press, 2007 and 2008 editions). Although the 12th Five Year Plan sets a goal of 5 GW for 2015 alone, for the sake of consistency this analysis uses the 2020 goal mentioned in the *China Solar PV Report*. The calculation is based on the 2007 China Input-Output Table with sectoral investment data provided by industry experts and surveys.

33. China Industrial Energy Efficiency and Clean Production Association, China Water Conservancy, and Hydro Power Press, *China's Energy Conservation and Emission Reduction Industry Development Report: Explore the Path of Low-carbon Economy* (Beijing: November 2010).

34. "National Energy Administration: 2010 New Wind Grid Connected Installed Capacity Was 13.99 Million Kilowatts, Top 2 in the World" (in Chinese), at www.cntronics.com/public/art/artinfo/id/80009644.

35. "Greenpeace: China Becomes World's Largest Wind-installation Country, Challenges Remain," *International Business Times*, 29 January 2011. Figure 5 from the following sources: NDRC, "China's Policies and Actions for Addressing Climate Change – Progress Report 2009" (Beijing: November 2009). 2009 data from REN21; 2010 data from *International Business Times* article, op. cit. this note.

36. *12th Five-Year Plan* (in Chinese), at www.gov.cn/2011lh/content_1825838.htm.

37. *Development Plan for Emerging New Energy Industry*, internal review draft. The official draft is scheduled for release during the first half of 2011.

Endnotes

38. In the 2007 China Input-Output Table, wind power generation is associated with the electricity and heat supply and generation industry. The wind turbine manufacturing industry is included as a subsector of the general and special equipment manufacturing industry. The wind technology R&D and maintenance service industry is associated with the scientific research industry and comprehensive technical services category.

39. Interview with Chinese wind industry expert Dr. Zhang Anhua, December 2010.

40. Table 3 based on the following sources: data on added wind capacity in 2006–09 from Li Junfeng et al., *China Wind Power Outlook 2010* (Hainan Province: Hainan Press, October 2010); data for 2010 derived from Greenpeace, "China Becomes World's Number 1 in Wind Installation," 12 January 2011, at www.greenpeace.org/eastasia/press/release/china-world-leader-wind-energy.

41. The 2020 goal of 120 GW is based on the high-development scenario in CREIA, *2008 China Wind Power Outlook*. The 12th Five-Year Plan, released in March 2011, set a wind development goal for 2015 close to 120 GW, but there is no official wind development goal for 2020. This report therefore uses the CREIA 2020 goal; however, this is subject to change as the 2020 goal is officially clarified in the future, meaning that future employment could increase significantly as well.

42. This estimation assumes that the 2020 goal for total installed wind capacity is 120 GW and that advancements in productivity will reduce the employment needs per unit of installed capacity by 38 percent between 2011 and 2020.

43. China's total installed wind capacity could reach as much as 253 GW by 2020, per CREIA, *China Wind Power Outlook 2010* (in Chinese), at http://download.chinagate.cn/ch/pdf/101014.pdf.

44. Multipliers obtained from the 2007 China Input-Output Table.

45. "Wind Power Equipment Price Changes When More Companies Are in the Market" (in Chinese), 31 October 2007, at www.86wind.com/info/detail/32-3554.html.

46. "Global Wind Turbine Needs Will Grow at 20% Compound Growth Rate" (in Chinese), www.51sole.com/Content.aspx?newsid=67578; "Jinfeng Technology Co. Bid With Low Price, Wind Turbine Cost Only 3000 yuan" (in Chinese), http://stock.stockstar.com/SN2010102730000181.shtml.

47. To estimate employment in Chinese wind turbine manufacturing, this study uses input-output analysis to calculate the scale of annual investment in the sector. The market price of a wind turbine unit is used to estimate the total production cost, which is then used as a proxy for total investment needed. This analysis uses the 2007 China Input-Output Table's direct and indirect employment multipliers for the wind turbine manufacturing sector (0.0097 and 0.0256 per 10,000 yuan of investment, respectively).Table 4 is based on the following sources: data on installed capacity of China's wind farms from Shi Pengfei, various years; 16 GW for 2010 from "China Installed Wind Capacity Is Top 1 in the World, More Than U.S," *Caijing*, 13 January 2011; 80 percent domestic share

for 2009 from projections in NDRC, *Development Plan for Emerging New Energy Industry*, draft.

Greening Transportation

1. "Year in Review: China's Ascent to Top of Global Auto Market," *China Daily*, 26 April 2010; Chinese Ministry of Environmental Protection, *China Vehicle Emission Control Annual Report 2010* (Beijing: November 2010), at www.vecc-mep.org.cn/index/20101110nianbao.pdf.

2. Data from International Energy Agency, 2008 Energy Balance for China and from U.S. Energy Information Agency, both available at http://grchina.com/gb/gbj/spot/spo06271.htm.

3. Vehicle production estimate is based on a regression analysis using historical data from the *China Statistical Yearbook* and from the *Economic Operation Report of China Industry, 2010*. According to the calculation, the cumulative total of new vehicles in 2011–20 is 255 million. However, with increasing in oil prices and rising popularity of public transportation, it is likely that the current exponential growth will not last. For ease of calculation, this report assumes that production and sales of fossil-fueled vehicles will maintain the same growth rate from 2011 to 2020. The number of new civilian vehicles in 2020 is estimated at 40 million, close to the forecast in the *Automobile Industry White Paper*. As a compromise, this report uses a figure for total automobile production from 2011 to 2020 of 222 million. However, this method results in a new vehicle estimate for 2010 of only 8.9 million, which is much lower than the actual production and sales figure of 18 million. Because automobile trade is generally balanced, exports are not considered in this report.

4. Anita Chang, "China's Massive Traffic Jam Could Last for Weeks," ABCNews.go.com, 24 August 2010.

5. Feng Xiang, "Investigation on the Massive Traffic Jam on the Tibet-Beijing Highway" (in Chinese), *Yunan Information Newspaper*, 16 September 2010.

6. Intercity railway investment data based on historical statistic reports released by the Statistical Center of the Ministry of Railway; urban rail investment data from "Urban Rail Investment in China's 25 Cities Amounts to 800 Billion Yuan," *Xinhua News*, www.chinaditie.com/news_show.asp?n_id=575.

7. Data for added value in the transportation sector are from *China Statistical Yearbook*. The added value in the rail sector is in line with the yearly investment in fixed assets reported in the Statistics Center of the Ministry of Railways' *Statistical Express* and *Statistical Bulletins*. No specific data were found for the rail transport sector. China reportedly invested some 200 billion yuan in urban rail transit construction during the 10th Five-Year Period, or 40 billion yuan per year, per "Total Planned Investment for Urban Rails in 25 Chinese Cities Reaches 800 Billion" (in Chinese), *Xinhua News*,18 July 2009, at www.chinaditie.com/news_show.asp?n_id=575.

8. China Statistics Press, *China Statistical Yearbook 2010* (Beijing: October 2010).

9. Based on data from the National Bureau of Statistics, at www.stats.gov.cn/tjsj/ndsj/2010/indexch.htm.

10. Ibid.

11. "Should We Be Happy About the Highest Automobile Sales in the World?" (in Chinese), *Jiefang Daily*, 12 January 2011.

12. "Project Ten Cities One Thousand Vehicles Launched" (in Chinese), http://news.xinhuanet.com/auto/2009-01/07/content_10615121.htm.

13. Ma Yang and Liu Jingyang, "China Needs New Energy Transportation System to Decrease Dependence on Oil," *Xinhua*, 21 July 2010.

14. "Subsidy Management for Pilot Program on Private Purchase of New Energy Vehicles" (in Chinese), www.sdpc.gov.cn/zcfb/zcfbqt/2010qt/t20100603_351147.htm.

15. Luo Sha and Yu Xiaojie, "China Electric Vehicle Production Will Reach 1 Million by 2020," *Xinhua News*, 18 October 2010.

16. This analysis uses three scenarios for new energy vehicle development, based on forecasts in the Fuel Efficient and Alternative Fuel Vehicle Industry Plan (2011–20) and from MOST and MIIT. Under the "low" development scenario (an R&D and promotion investment of 200 billion yuan), the cumulative production of new energy vehicles (hybrid and electric combined) is 10.5 million during 2011–20, and new energy vehicles account for 6 percent of new car production and sales by 2020. Under the "medium" scenario (investment of 300 billion yuan), cumulative production is 22.2 million, and new energy vehicles account for 10 percent of production. Under the "high" scenario (investment of 400 billion yuan), cumulative production is 33.3 million, and new energy vehicles account for 15 percent of production. To derive an estimate of the total investment needed, we assume an average unit cost during the 2011–20 period of 80,000 yuan for electric vehicles and 150,000 yuan for hybrid vehicles. These costs are based on a survey of new energy vehicle prices in China's current market (see http://news.51auto.com/201007/ct25069.htm, in Chinese). Over the coming decade, R&D breakthroughs, facility upgrades, and increases in investment and promotion should lower the unit cost to equal that of fossil fuel vehicles. If we convert the projected production volumes to total investment, this would result in new energy vehicle investments during 2011–20 of 1.39 trillion, 2.85 trillion, and 4.23 trillion yuan, respectively, under the low, medium, and high development scenarios. To derive the direct and indirect employment effects of this investment, we use coefficients from the 2007 Input-Output Table, with "Science Research" serving as a proxy for "R&D, Promotion and Investment," and "Transport Facility Manufacturing" serving as a proxy for "Hybrid Passenger Vehicle and Electric Vehicle Production."

17. "China Rail Operation Mileage Top 2, High Speed Rail Operation Mileage Top 1" (in Chinese), *Chinanews*, 4 March 2011, at http://industry.fivip.com/indtrend/20110304/3626502.html.

18. Ministry of Railways, *Medium and Long-Term Railway Network Plan (adjusted in 2008)* (in Chinese), www.china-mor.gov.cn/tljs/tlgh/201012/t20101228_731.html.

19. In China's long-term HSR development plan, "Four Horizontal and Four Vertical" investment is 110.3 million yuan per kilometer, and cross-region HSR investment is 112.7 million yuan per kilometer. This report uses the average of these two numbers, or 111.7 million yuan. The investment structure estimate is derived by breaking down total investment into categories that correspond to the 2007 China Input-Output Table, as follows: 5 percent for "communications, signal and information engineering," which corresponds to "communications equipment, computer services and other electronic equipment manufacturing"; 5 percent for "electricity and electric traction," which corresponds to "electricity and thermal production and supply"; 15 percent for "train purchase" (higher than the predicted ratio), which corresponds to "transportation equipment manufacturing"; and 75 percent for "infrastructure investment," which corresponds to "building industry."

20. The direct and indirect employment effect is calculated based on investments in the individual categories and application of the relevant employment coefficients in the 2007 China Input-Output Table. Total job creation also includes incurred employment; international and domestic experience shows that HSR could stimulate real estate development along the rail line, as well as tourism, hotels, and retail development. Indirect jobs will be created in these sectors. Because of insufficient data to estimate indirect job creation, the report does not discuss this.

21. Based on volume data from the *Chinese Urban Development Statistic Yearbook 2002-2007*, as cited in the *Urban Rail Transit Research Report*, internal research document.

22. Ibid.

23. China Architecture and Building Press, *Chinese Urban Development Statistic Yearbook 2002-2007*.

24. "2010 Nationwide Urban Rail Transportation Index" (in Chinese), at www.chinautc.com/information/news show.asp?newsid=3304.

25. "2010 China Urban Rail Key Technology Forum Is Held in Shanghai" (in Chinese), 11 November 2010, http://finance.sina.com.cn/roll/20101111/12493516532.shtml.

26. "Shanghai's Metro and London's Tube Head to Head," Bricoleurbanism.org, 25 July 2010.

27. "Chinese Subway Receives 200 Billion Yuan Investment During the 10th Five-Year Period" (in Chinese), *People's Daily*, 18 January 2002.

28. "Economic Features and System Mode of Urban Rail Transport" (in Chinese), at www.interscm.com/info/delivery/200806/09-31708.html.

29. "Total Planned Investment…," op. cit. note 7.

30. It is not clear exactly how much has been invested in these green transport sectors in recent years; however, it is relatively easier to estimate the future employment effect using input-output analysis because the scale of future investment is basically consistent with the government development plan and has no variations.

31. "Beijing to Invest 500 Billion Yuan to Establish Urban Metro Net," *Beijing Daily*, 29 December 2010. The total mileage will increase from 278 kilometers in 2010 to 660 kilometers during 2011–15. Total investment will be 500

Endnotes

billion yuan, or an average investment of 1.31 billion yuan per kilometer. This dynamic investment figure is very different from the static investment figure of 400–500 million yuan, which is calculated by using the real investment. Considering the actual situation, future investment will be estimated by dynamic investment. Thus, from 2016 to 2020, Beijing will have 340 more kilometers of rail transportation, at a total investment of 445 billion yuan.

32. Table 5 based on calculations of the future investment and employment effect of Beijing's urban rail development plan. This report uses investment structure estimates for urban rail system development during the two five-year periods of 2011–15 and 2016–20 and then breaks down these investments to correspond with the relevant categories of employment coefficients in the 2007 China Input-Output Table.

Greening the Forestry Sector

1. Biodiversity Clearing-House Mechanism of China, *Biodiversity in China* (in Chinese), available at www.biodiv.gov.cn/images_biodiv/ecosystems/forests-zh.htm.

2. Figure 6 from *China Forestry Yearbook 2006–2010* (Beijing: China Forestry Press). Data cover all forestry products including timber and non-timber industries.

3. Calculation is based on the current average growth rate.

4. State Forestry Administration (SFA), *Results of the 7th National Forest Resource Survey* (in Chinese), 28 January 2010, at www.forestry.gov.cn/portal/main/s/65/content-326341.html.

5. Ge Quansheng et al., "Statistical Analysis of China's Forest Resource and Precipitation in the Past 50 Years," *Journal of Natural Resources*, September 2001.

6. SFA, op. cit. note 4.

7. Figure 7 from the Development Research Center of the State Council of China. Note that before 1985, forestation was "counted" once the survival rate reaches 40 percent; after 1985, the ratio was raised to 85 percent. According to forestation technical specification GB/T 15776-2006, since 2006, this dataset has included closed-off areas of non-forest land and partial forest land as part of the total forestation area.

8. SFA, "Forest Coverage Increases from 8.6% to 18.21%" (in Chinese), at www.gov.cn/wszb/zhibo354/content_1465687.htm.

9. SFA, *China Forestry Development Report 2010* (in Chinese), at www.forestry.gov.cn/portal/main/s/62/content-464039.html.

10. On February 27, 1982, the State Council issued the National Implementation Measures for the Compulsory Tree-Planting Campaign. Since then, compulsory tree planting has become the responsibility of every Chinese citizen who has reached the appropriate age. See "2009 Greening the Land Bulletin" (in Chinese), www.jiadinglife.cn/news/xwjd/2010-03-12/10667.html.

11. National Development and Reform Commission, "China's National Climate Change Program" (Beijing: June 2007), at www.ccchina.gov.cn/WebSite/CCChina/UpFile/File188.pdf.

12. Ibid.

13. Ibid.

14. Ibid.

15. Wei Xiaoshuang, "Great Ecological Achievement in the Last 60 Years" (in Chinese), *People's Daily*, 26 September 2010, at www.qstheory.cn/st/stwm/201009/t20100926_50342.htm.

16. "How Much Is China's Forestry Worth?" (in Chinese), *People's Daily*, 25 May 2010.

17. Ibid.

18. *China Forestry Statistical Yearbook 2009* (Beijing: China Forestry Press, June 2010).

19. SFA, *Cost Estimation Standard for Shelter-forest Forestation Project*, January 2009.

20. Table 6 uses the following formula to calculate the direct employment effect of afforestation activities: Direct job creation=(Working time needed per unit area of forestation × yearly forestation area)/Standard annual working days for a typical full-time job.

21. Multipliers are from the 2007 China Input-Output Table.

22. "Hu Jintao's Speech on Climate Change," *New York Times*, 22 September 2009.

23. The methodology used to derive future projections is modified slightly to better simulate the actual effect. In long-term forestation planning, there is concern about the survivability of previously planted trees. Assuming a 100-percent survivability rate for simple calculation purposes, the new forest area would be equal to the new forestation area. As technology development and forest management improve, productivity will also increase. Assuming an average productivity increase of 3 percent annually, the formula used to calculate job creation from afforestation in year n (n>2010) is: New job creation in year n = (total time spend on new forestation (in days)/300 days) × $(1\text{-}3\%)^{n\text{-}2010}$.

24. *China Forestry Statistical Yearbook 2009*, op. cit. note 18.

25. SFA, *Assessment Index for Forestation Project Investment* (in Chinese), 19 November 2008, at www.law-lib.com/law/law_view.asp?id=270574.

26. Table 7 based on ibid.

27. There is no specific category of "forest management" in the 2007 China Input-Output Table. The closest relevant category is "water conservancy, environmental and public management" which has an indirect employment multiplier of 1.475.

28. As with forestation activity, this estimate assumes a 100-percent survivability rate.

29. Author interviews with Chinese forestry expert Dr. Shuifa Ke, Beijing Forestry University.

30. *China Forestry Statistical Yearbook 2009*, op. cit. note 18.

31. Figure 8 from Chinese Academy of Social Sciences, Institute of Urban Development and Environment, *Low Carbon Development and Green Jobs in China*.

32. Due to data limitations, projections are used to estimate sectoral revenue and employment figures for 2009 and 2010. For 2009, the estimated revenue was 22.5–23.4 billion yuan and the jobs estimate was 155,000 direct jobs. Because of the unavailability of crucial data required by Input-Output Modeling estimates, such as annual investment in forest park tourism, this report uses scenario analysis to project revenue and then uses employment elasticity over revenue to estimate the direct employment effect. Based on the historical data provided in Figure 8, we could derive an average of 0.40 elasticity of employment over revenue. From 1998 to 2008, China's forest park tourism revenue experienced average annual growth of 37.6 percent. To calculate direct employment creation from forest park tourism, this study relies on three scenarios for revenue growth and employment for 2008 onward: a high-growth scenario of 25 percent average growth in annual revenue from 2009–15 and 20 percent from 2016–20; a moderate-growth scenario of 20 percent average growth for the entire period 2009–20; and a low-growth scenario of 20 percent average from 2009–15 and 10 percent average growth from 2016 onward.

33. Because there is no specific forest park tourism category in the 2007 China Input-Output Table, this study uses data for the overall tourism sector. Chinese statistics categorize tourism income data into six sectors: transportation and storage, postal industry, wholesale and retail,

accommodation and catering, residential services and other services, and the culture, sports, and entertainment industry. Calculations for China's 2007 tourism income was analyzed under related service sectors, with results indicating that 1.95 million direct jobs were created and another 3.03 million jobs could be created through the service industry chain, i.e. every direct job created in tourism would create 1.55 jobs in other relevant sectors. Applying these calculations enables calculations of direct and indirect jobs in forest park tourism in 2009 and 2010.

Accelerating China's Green Transition

1. For details on China's wind development, see , "Beyond the Numbers: A Closer Look at China's Wind Power Success," *ReVolt* (Worldwatch Institute blog), 28 February 2011.

2. "Solar PV Industry Leaves Pollution in China?" *Southern Weekend*, 23 July 2010, available at http://energy .people.com.cn/GB/12231525.html.

3. "Energy Saving Assessment and Evaluation Face Statistical Difficulties" (in Chinese), available at www .ccchina.gov.cn/cn/NewsInfo.asp?NewsId=27890.

4. See Haibing Ma and Lini Fu, "Green Design Faces Gray Reality for China's 'Eco-Cities,'" *ReVolt* (Worldwatch Institute blog), 27 January 2011.

Index

Index

hybrid-electric vehicles, 17
Hyundai, 8

I

implementation plans, systemic, 27
initiatives, energy, 9
Inner Mongolia, 12, 16
institutional mechanisms, building, 26
International Energy Agency, 10
investing, green, 27

J

job creation, *see* green jobs

L

Lee Myung-Bak, 8
Li Keqiang, 7

M

manufacturing sector
    initiatives in, 9
    solar photovoltaics, 12–13, 13t
    wind turbine, 14–15
market-based incentives, 26

N

National Arbor Day, 21
National Climate Change (program), 21
Ningxia province, 12

P

photovoltaics. *see* solar photovoltaics
policy implementation, 26
pollution types, 7–8
public education campaign, 27

Q

Qinghai province, 12

R

railway network plan (long term), 18
reforestation, defined, 20–21
renewable energy, 10–11
research and development, 26

S

Samsung, 8
sandstorms, controlling source, 21
Shanghai, 18
Shanxi province, 16

Six Key Forestry Projects, 21
solar photovoltaics
    capacity, 13f, 14t
    defined, 12
    green transition and, 25
    manufacturing considerations, 12–13, 13t
    power generation, 13
    solar radiation map, 12f
solar power-generation technologies, 12
solar water heating, 11–12, 11f
South Korea, 8
State Environmental Protection Agency (SEPA), 8
State Forestry Administration (SFA), 20
Statistical Yearbook, 17

T

"Ten Cities, One Thousand Vehicles," 17
Tianjin, 21
tourism
    forestry sector, 24
    initiatives for, 9
    jobs and revenue, 24f
transportation
    alternative fuel vehicles, 17
    energy consumption and, 16
    greening overview, 16–17
    high-speed rail, 17–18
    initiatives for, 9
    job creation, 17–19
    urban rail, 18–19

U

United Nations Environment Programme (UNEP), 9
urban rail, 18–19, 19t

W

waste/water initiatives, 9
water pollution, 8
wind power
    capacity, 14f, 14t, 25
    defined, 13
    employment opportunities, 15t
    generating, 14
    wind turbine manufacturing, 14–15
World Health Organization, 7

X

Xinjiang province, 12
Xizang province (Tibet), 12

Worldwatch Reports provide in-depth, quantitative, and qualitative analysis of the major issues affecting prospects for a sustainable society. The Reports are written by members of the Worldwatch Institute research staff or outside specialists and are reviewed by experts unaffiliated with Worldwatch. They are used as concise and authoritative references by governments, nongovernmental organizations, and educational institutions worldwide.

On Climate Change, Energy, and Materials

184: Powering the Low-Carbon Economy: The Once and Future Roles of Renewable Energy and Natural Gas
183: Population, Climate Change, and Women's Lives
182: Renewable Energy and Energy Efficiency in China: Current Status and Prospects for 2020
178: Low-Carbon Energy: A Roadmap, 2008
175: Powering China's Development: the Role of Renewable Energy, 2007
169: Mainstreaming Renewable Energy in the 21st Century, 2004
160: Reading the Weathervane: Climate Policy From Rio to Johannesburg, 2002
157: Hydrogen Futures: Toward a Sustainable Energy System, 2001
151: Micropower: The Next Electrical Era, 2000
149: Paper Cuts: Recovering the Paper Landscape, 1999
144: Mind Over Matter: Recasting the Role of Materials in Our Lives, 1998
138: Rising Sun, Gathering Winds: Policies To Stabilize the Climate and Strengthen Economies, 1997

On Ecological and Human Health

181: Global Environmental Change: The Threat to Human Health
174: Oceans in Peril: Protecting Marine Biodiversity, 2007
165: Winged Messengers: The Decline of Birds, 2003
153: Why Poison Ourselves: A Precautionary Approach to Synthetic Chemicals, 2000
148: Nature's Cornucopia: Our Stakes in Plant Diversity, 1999
145: Safeguarding the Health of Oceans, 1999
142: Rocking the Boat: Conserving Fisheries and Protecting Jobs, 1998
141: Losing Strands in the Web of Life: Vertebrate Declines and the Conservation of Biological Diversity, 1998
140: Taking a Stand: Cultivating a New Relationship With the World's Forests, 1998

On Economics, Institutions, and Security

177: Green Jobs: Working for People and the Environment, 2008
173: Beyond Disasters: Creating Opportunities for Peace, 2007
168: Venture Capitalism for a Tropical Forest: Cocoa in the Mata Atlântica, 2003
167: Sustainable Development for the Second World: Ukraine and the Nations in Transition, 2003
166: Purchasing Power: Harnessing Institutional Procurement for People and the Planet, 2003
164: Invoking the Spirit: Religion and Spirituality in the Quest for a Sustainable World, 2002
162: The Anatomy of Resource Wars, 2002
159: Traveling Light: New Paths for International Tourism, 2001
158: Unnatural Disasters, 2001

On Food, Water, Population, and Urbanization

176: Farming Fish for the Future, 2008
172: Catch of the Day: Choosing Seafood for Healthier Oceans, 2007
171: Happer Meals: Rethinking the Global Meat Industry, 2005
170: Liquid Assets: The Critical Need to Safeguard Freshwater Ecosytems, 2005
163: Home Grown: The Case for Local Food in a Global Market, 2002
161: Correcting Gender Myopia: Gender Equity, Women's Welfare, and the Environment, 2002
156: City Limits: Putting the Brakes on Sprawl, 2001
154: Deep Trouble: The Hidden Threat of Groundwater Pollution, 2000
150: Underfed and Overfed: The Global Epidemic of Malnutrition, 2000
147: Reinventing Cities for People and the Planet, 1999

To see a complete list of our Reports, visit www.worldwatch.org/taxonomy/term/40